What Are Spiritual Gifts?

Basics of the Faith

How Do We Glorify God?
How Our Children Come to Faith
What Are Election and Predestination?
What Are Spiritual Gifts?
What Is a Reformed Church?
What Is a True Calvinist?
What Is Biblical Preaching?
What Is Church Government?
What Is Hell?
What Is Justification by Faith Alone?
What Is Perseverance of the Saints?
What Is Providence?
What Is Spiritual Warfare?
What Is the Atonement?
What Is the Christian Worldview?
What Is the Lord's Supper?
What Is True Conversion?
What Is Vocation?
What Is Worship Music?
Why Do We Baptize Infants?

What Are Spiritual Gifts?

Vern S. Poythress

P&R
PUBLISHING
P.O. BOX 817 • PHILLIPSBURG • NEW JERSEY 08865-0817

Italics within Scripture quotations indicate emphasis added.

Parts of this booklet have been taken from Vern S. Poythress, "Modern Spiritual Gifts as Analogous to Apostolic Gifts: Affirming Extraordinary Works of the Spirit within Cessationist Theology," *Journal of the Evangelical Theological Society* 39/1 (1996): 71–101, available at <http://www.frame-poythress.org/poythress_articles/1996Modern.htm>. Used with permission.

Page design by Tobias Design

Printed in the United States of America

Library of Congress Cataloging-in-Publication Data

Poythress, Vern S.
What are spiritual gifts? / Vern S. Poythress.
p. cm. -- (Basics of the faith)
Includes bibliographical references.
ISBN 978-1-59638-209-1 (pbk.)
1. Gifts, Spiritual. I. Title.
BT767.3.P67 2010
234'.13--dc22

2010024684

What are spiritual gifts?

The Bible indicates in several places that God equips and empowers people for service within the church, which is the body of Christ. Since God is the source for our abilities, these empowerments may be called "gifts" from God. In the chart on the following page are five lists of types of gifts, taken from different passages. No one of the lists includes all gifts. The list in 1 Peter 4:11 contains only two, speaking and serving. But these two labels can cover a broad spectrum of activities. The more detailed lists give us a sampling of the kinds of service that God brings about among the people in the church.

SOME BASIC CHARACTERISTICS OF SPIRITUAL GIFTS

First Corinthians 12 gives a more extended discussion of gifts than the other passages. Several points stand out.

- Every person who trusts in Christ for salvation belongs to Christ and so belongs to the church, the body of Christ. ("Now you are the body of Christ and individually members of it" [1 Cor. 12:27].) God does not want Christians to live in isolation, but as part of his special community, the church.

Romans 12:6–8	1 Corinthians 12:8–10	1 Corinthians 12:28–30	Ephesians 4:11	1 Peter 4:11
		apostles	apostles	speaking
prophecy	prophecy	prophets	prophets	
teaching	utterance of wisdom	teachers	teachers*	
exhorting	utterance of knowledge		pastors	
			evangelists	
leading		administrating		
	working miracles	working miracles		
	gifts of healing	gifts of healing		
service		helping		serving
doing acts of mercy				
contributing (money)				
	faith			
	distinguishing spirits			
	speaking in tongues	speaking in tongues		
	interpretation of tongues	interpretation of tongues		

* Some interpreters think that "pastors" and "teachers" are two labels for the same persons, "pastor-teachers."

- Each person in the church is like one member of a human body. God appoints each person to have a function in the body (1 Cor. 12:12).
- Each person has his own function in the body; not all are the same (1 Cor. 12:14–25).
- The Holy Spirit empowers each person to serve according to what God wills (1 Cor. 12:11).
- The whole body, the church, suffers if one member suffers (1 Cor. 12:26). Given the concern in 1 Cor. 12 for the functions of different members, the verse seems to imply that the body may suffer partly because one member is not carrying out its functions, which help the whole body.
- The whole body flourishes when one member is honored (1 Cor. 12:26).

In our modern context, just calling a group a church does not make it so in God's eyes. A true church functions according to God's design, which includes many aspects. Among them are the practice of Christian love (1 Cor. 13), sound doctrine (the church is to be in fellowship with the *apostles*, who were commissioned with Christ's authority), and purity in life (1 Cor. 5:6-8). Sound doctrine implies preaching based on the Bible, and purity implies the exercise of church discipline. But on earth, no church is perfect. It is composed of people who have been redeemed from their sins by Christ, but who still struggle against remaining sin.

THE BASIS FOR GIFTS IN THE TRINITY

The biblical descriptions of spiritual gifts show their close relation to God who gives them. The doctrine of the

Trinity, as found in the Bible, teaches that there is only one true God, and that God exists in three persons, the Father, the Son, and the Holy Spirit. We can see the participation of the persons of the Godhead in the operation of spiritual gifts in 1 Corinthians 12:4–6:

> Now there are varieties of gifts, but the same Spirit [the Holy Spirit, the third person of the Trinity]; and there are varieties of service, but the same Lord [the Son, the second person of the Trinity]; and there are varieties of activities, but it is the same God [the Father] who empowers them all in everyone.

God the Father empowers all the services. The services take place in the body of *Christ*. And the *Holy Spirit* apportions gifts to each (1 Cor. 12:11). All three persons of the Godhead are active. The gifts are called "spiritual" (Greek *pneumatika*) because the Holy Spirit gives and empowers them. They are called "gifts" (Greek *charismata*) because God gives them by grace, rather than our having to earn them.

Each person who belongs to Christ has the Holy Spirit dwelling within him:

> You, however, are not in the flesh but in the Spirit, if in fact the Spirit of God dwells in you. Anyone who does not have the Spirit of Christ does not belong to him. But if Christ is in you, although the body is dead because of sin, the Spirit is life because of righteousness. (Rom. 8:9–10)

Each Christian, by being united to Christ, receives the Holy Spirit as the one central gift from God (Acts 2:33, 38; Gal. 3:14). The Holy Spirit then distributes particular gifts, which differ from one person to another: "All these [gifts] are empowered by one and the same Spirit, who apportions to each one individually as he wills" (1 Cor. 12:11).

ONE-STAGE OR TWO-STAGE CHRISTIANITY?

The two things—having the Holy Spirit and having his gifts—go together. Anyone who is united to Christ is united to the *whole* of Christ. If you come to Christ, you come to personal fellowship with him, and that fellowship is the basis for all the benefits of salvation, including spiritual gifts. We do not *earn* the privilege of having spiritual gifts by going through some special additional steps. The gifts of the Spirit are gifts of grace, not merited by us but given freely out of God's bounty. Spiritual gifts are gifts from Christ (Eph. 4:7–8, 11).

The same point comes out in 1 Corinthians 12. The only way to become part of the church is by being a member of the body (verses 12–13). Each member has some function, some gift (verses 18–26). No member is dispensable (verses 21–23).

This principle of membership is important because some people are confused about it. Some people claim that the coming of the Holy Spirit is a two-stage rather than a one-stage process. They agree that the Holy Spirit dwells in every Christian believer. But they claim that there is still a second stage, which they often call "baptism with the Holy Spirit," which gives a Christian for the first time a special empowerment for service and a special equipping with gifts of the Spirit.

The biggest trouble with this theory in its usual form is that it contradicts 1 Corinthians 12. It implies that there are two classes of Christians, some with special gifts and some without. The ones with special gifts are clearly the best. The distinction between the two classes divides the body of Christ, and tempts people to despise the alleged inferior class of nonspiritual Christians.

The distinction directly opposes the point in 1 Corinthians 12, that every member of the body has a positive contribution and is to be appreciated for that contribution.

Why then has such an erroneous theory developed? The book of Acts does indicate that the coming of the Holy Spirit at Pentecost resulted in a radical change. This was an epoch-changing event for the whole church, for the whole people of God, not just for some individuals. Before Pentecost, the Holy Spirit had been quietly active in people's lives. But only *after* Jesus finished his work and ascended to the Father did the Holy Spirit come in a new way, bringing the full benefits of Jesus' work that was now fully accomplished. "Being therefore exalted at the right hand of God, and having received from the Father the promise of the Holy Spirit, he [Jesus] has poured out this that you yourselves are seeing and hearing [the work of the Spirit on the day of Pentecost]" (Acts 2:33). Clearly this change at Pentecost is important. But it is a mistake to make it a point of division *within the church today*, rather than a division between the time before and after Christ completed his work.

GROWTH

The theory of two stages for spiritual gifts also has an attraction because Christians can indeed grow after they are converted. The growth can be gradual, or it can come in spurts and in crises. After a crisis, a Christian may look back and feel as if he has undergone a black-and-white change from lacking spiritual power to having spiritual power. What do we say about such experiences? The Holy Spirit works as he wills (1 Cor. 12:11). We can affirm the reality of many of these crisis experiences, while at the same time not despising those whose growth is more gradual and less dramatic.

The Bible includes affirmations of the importance of growth. The picture in 1 Corinthians 12 implies that individual members and the body as a whole can grow (see Eph. 4:11–16). Members are not expected to sit passively, knowing they are part of the body of Christ. They are to participate; they are to interact and serve each other. They are continually to be "filled with the Spirit" (Eph. 5:18). In Acts we see the Holy Spirit filling the apostles individually or filling the church for the purpose of speaking God's Word (Acts 4:8, 31; 6:3, 10; 7:55; 13:9). The Bible tells Christians that we should "earnestly desire the spiritual gifts," which implies that we may receive more gifts over time, or the Holy Spirit may deepen gifts that we already have (1 Cor. 14:1).

At a principial level, we have all that we need when we have Christ. He is all-sufficient (1 Cor. 1:30). Through him we have the Holy Spirit, who indwells us and empowers us (Rom. 8:9–11). But this truth should not make us complacent. We should earnestly and actively seek to serve Christ with more consistency and fervor. We should "earnestly desire the spiritual gifts" as part of our zeal to serve him. In principle, Christian growth, including growth in spiritual gifts, can involve many stages, not just two. But all the "stages," if that is what we call them, are based on the one initial gift, where God unites us to Christ and gives us the Spirit of Christ. It is up to the Spirit, not to us, to decide when and how he brings a variety of experiences into any person's life.

In practical terms, we are to seek Christ, and all he has to give, and then to serve his people. In so doing, gifts will come to light.

CHRIST-CENTERED CHARACTER OF GIFTS

What kinds of gifts should we be seeking to exercise? The lists of gifts given in New Testament passages offer a starting point. But none of the lists is exhaustive. We need a broad biblical framework for thinking about gifts of the Holy Spirit.

The New Testament provides this framework. One key passage is Ephesians 4:7–11. Jesus Christ is head of the church and distributor of all gifts of the Spirit (verse 11). He distributes gifts from the fullness that he possesses, because he has triumphed (verse 8) and fills all things (verse 10). Acts 2:33 supplements this picture by saying that Christ "received from the Father the promise of the Holy Spirit" as a prelude to pouring out the Spirit on the church. From Christ's fullness of the Spirit we receive a measure, "according to the measure of Christ's gift" (Eph. 4:7).

These reflections naturally lead to the conclusion that our ministry in the Spirit is analogous to, as well as subordinate to, the ministry of Christ. For example, Christ is the final great prophet (Acts 3:22–26). Through the pouring out of the Spirit at Pentecost, we all become subordinate prophets (Acts 2:17–18). Christ is the chief shepherd (1 Peter 5:4), the ruler over the church. Through the Spirit he appoints subordinate shepherds (Acts 20:28; 1 Peter 5:1–3) and gives gifts of ruling and administering and caring for the flock (1 Cor. 12:28; Eph. 4:11 "pastors"). Christ came to serve and give his life as a ransom for many (Matt. 20:28). He also gives gifts of service (Rom. 12:7–8) and calls on us "to lay down our lives for the brothers" (1 John 3:16).

The work of Christ for us can be conveniently classified under the traditional triad of biblical offices: prophet, king, and priest. Christ speaks to us (prophet), he rules over us (king), and he gives his life in service for us (priest). All three functions occur together in Hebrews 1:1–3. When we are united to Christ, we are transformed into his likeness and bear his image (Rom. 8:29; 2 Cor. 3:18; Eph. 4:24). We become prophets who speak his Word to others (Col. 3:16; 4:6). We become kings who exercise authority in his name over the areas for which we are responsible (Eph. 2:6; 6:4). We become priests who serve one another (1 John 3:16).

The relevant scriptural passages show that these things are true for everyone who believes in Christ. But not everyone is equally gifted in every area (Eph. 4:7). Where speaking gifts are strong, people become recognized as teachers (Eph. 4:11). Where ruling gifts are strong, people become recognized as elders or shepherds (1 Peter 5:1–4). Where serving gifts are strong, people become recognized as servers and givers of mercy. Some suggest that we may correlate this service with the ministry of deacons (the key Greek word *diakonos*, translated *deacon*, means *servant*).

The three categories of prophetic, kingly, and priestly gifts are not rigidly separated from one another. Both in Christ's life and in the lives of his people there are typically combinations. For example, pastoring involves both providing nourishment for sheep through the Word of Christ (a prophetic function) and leading and protecting the sheep (a kingly function).

All the gifts mentioned in Romans 12, 1 Corinthians 12, and Ephesians 4 may be roughly classified as prophetic, kingly, or priestly. For example, gifts of wisdom and knowledge are prophetic, while gifts of administration, miraculous powers, and healing are kingly. But some gifts could easily be classified in more than one way. For example, healing could be seen as priestly, since it is an exercise of mercy toward the person healed. Ultimately, prophetic, kingly, and priestly functions may be expanded into perspectives on the whole life of God's people, so we should not be disturbed by the apparent overlap. This classification is nevertheless useful in reminding us of our relation to the work of Christ and in reminding us that no single list of gifts in the New Testament is intended to be exhaustive.

A PYRAMID OF GIFTEDNESS

Because the gifts have varying functions and intensities, the New Testament recognizes several levels of functioning for prophetic, kingly, and priestly gifts (see Figure 1). What are they?

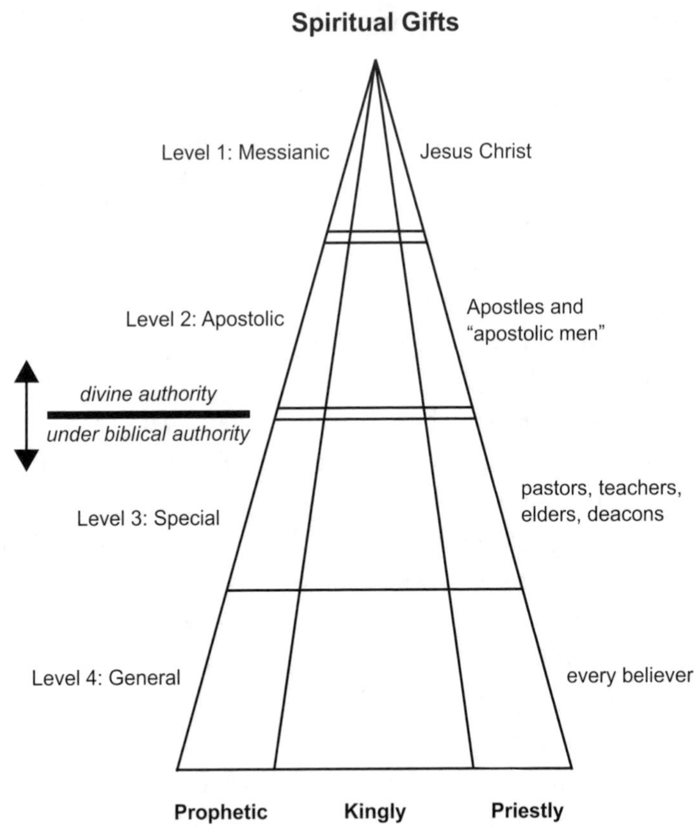

First and foremost, there is messianic giftedness (level 1). Christ alone has a fullness of the Spirit to equip him as final prophet, king, and priest in a definitive way.

Second, there is apostolic or foundational giftedness (level 2). Christ appointed the apostles as witnesses (Acts

1:21–22). On the basis of what they had directly seen and heard, and on the basis of the work of the Holy Spirit inspiring them, they could testify authoritatively for all time concerning what Christ accomplished. In their verbal witness, they had an unrepeatable prophetic role. The apostles and closely associated "apostolic men," including Mark, Luke, and Jude, wrote the books of the New Testament.

Similarly, the apostles made foundational decisions concerning the rule or shepherding of the New Testament church. They led it through its first crises (Acts 6; 8; 10–11; 15; 20). Thus they had an unrepeatable kingly role. The apostles appointed the first deacons and so stabilized the ministry of service and mercy (Acts 6:1–7). In all these areas the role of the apostles is *unrepeatable*.

Third, we have the level of prominent, *repeatable* gifts (level 3). People may be officially recognized by the church when they have strong gifts in teaching, ruling, and giving mercy. Traditionally, Reformed thinking about the church has designated this level "special office." It includes the teachers, elders, and deacons in the church (Phil. 1:1; 1 Tim. 3:1–13; 5:17).

Finally, we have the level of involvement of every believer (level 4). As Scripture shows, every believer united to Christ is made a prophet, a king, and a priest in a broad sense.

The distinction between gifts with full divine authority and subordinate (uninspired) gifts is now clear. Jesus Christ is God (John 1:1; 20:28) and is the Lord of the church (Eph. 5:24). His work has full divine authority. The apostles and apostolic men are commissioned by Christ and bear his authority. Hence their words and official actions have divine authority (see, e.g., 1 Cor. 14:37; 1 Thess. 2:13). In particular, words of the apostles in the exercise of their office are "inspired" in the technical sense. "Inspired" words are those spoken by God and breathed out by God (2 Tim. 3:16); hence they carry unqualified divine authority.

The Holy Spirit also works in a subordinate way in giving teaching and speaking gifts to pastors, teachers, and ordinary believers (Eph. 4:11; Col. 4:6). The speeches that these people give are not inspired. That is, the speeches are not identically the speech of God in such a way that they carry unqualified divine authority and perfection.

Such speeches may nevertheless be "inspiring" in the popular sense of the word. We thank God for the gifts that are exercised, and we know that when properly exercised they come from the power of the Spirit. The Holy Spirit is present and blesses us through sermons and exhortations from fellow believers. But the messages are always fallible and must be checked by the standard of the Bible. The necessity of testing later works by the Scriptures is implied by the finality of revelation in Christ (Heb. 1:1–3), the foundational character of the teaching of the apostles (Eph. 2:20), and the fact that the canon of Scripture is complete.

RECIPIENTS OF SERVICE IN GIFTS

If we wish, we can expand our discussion of spiritual gifts by making still more distinctions. For example, we can ask who is being served. Is a particular gift serving God, the church, or the world? In a sense, any gift serves God. And a gift that promotes the spiritual health of the church also helps the church serve the world. But we can still see distinct foci in kinds of service. Prayer and praise serve God. Gifts of instruction and administration within the church serve the church. Evangelistic communication serves the world.

Some gifts, such as teaching, can easily function either toward the church or toward the world or toward both. A college instructor who teaches about Christian faith in a secular college is serving the world. When the same person teaches a Sunday school class, he serves the church. Similarly with ministry of mercy. Deacons can help people in physical or financial distress, both members of the church and people who are not. We have a special obligation toward fellow Christians: "So then, as we have opportunity, let us do good to everyone, and *especially* to those who are of the household of faith" (Gal. 6:10). But the biblical principle, "You shall love your neighbor as yourself" (Gal. 5:14), implies service to non-Christians as well. The Christian who teaches chemistry or economics ought to be motivated by Christian love, to be empowered by the Holy Spirit, and to serve God and not man (Eph. 6:6–8). Similarly, the Christian businessman should endeavor to treat his employees kindly and fairly, and to offer a good product at a fair price. In this sense, "gifts" may be exercised quite broadly. How should Christians exercise gifts in relation to the world as a whole? The question of our relation to the world deserves attention, but is beyond the scope of our discussion. In this booklet we concentrate on gifts serving the church.

WHICH GIFTS ARE UNIQUE TO THE APOSTLES?

People debate which gifts within the New Testament still function today, and which have ceased because they were unique to the apostles and their associates. That is an important question. But we have to be careful about how we pose the question. Figure 1 on page 14, about kinds of gifts, clearly suggests that several kinds of function—prophetic, kingly, and priestly gifts—continue to this day. Christ is the source of all the gifts. When people are united to him, they become prophets, kings, and priests—all three.

APOSTOLIC AUTHORITY

But our gifts today are not on the same *level* as those of Christ and his apostles. That is an important distinction for us to consider. The debate about which gifts are continuing is really asking about the unique status and authority that belonged to the apostles. With the apostles we should also group some of their associates such as Mark and Luke whom God inspired to write the two Gospels with their names. The apostles were uniquely commissioned by Christ, so that what they say has Christ's own authority:

> Whoever receives you receives me, and whoever receives me receives him who sent me. (Matt. 10:40)

> If anyone thinks that he is a prophet, or spiritual, he should acknowledge that the things I am writing to you are a command of the Lord. (1 Cor. 14:37)

Why this unique authority? God has worked out eternal redemption in Christ, who is himself the climactic revelation of God:

> Long ago, at many times and in many ways, God spoke to our fathers by the prophets, but in these last days he has spoken to us by his Son, whom he appointed the heir of all things, through whom also he created the world. (Heb. 1:1–2)

The revelation given in Christ and in his appointed apostolic interpreters is never to be superseded or surpassed.

Accordingly, the New Testament speaks of a fixed "deposit" of teaching that is to be kept and taught:

> Follow the pattern of the sound words that you have heard from me, in the faith and love that are in Christ Jesus. By the Holy Spirit who dwells within us, guard the good *deposit* entrusted to you. (2 Tim. 1:13–14)

The Revelation of John specifically forbids adding or subtracting from it:

> I warn everyone who hears the words of the prophecy of this book: if anyone *adds to them*, God will add to him the plagues described in this book, and if anyone *takes away from the words of the book of this prophecy*, God will take away his share in the tree of life and in the holy city, which are described in this book. (Rev. 22:18–19)

Revelation thereby puts itself in the same category with the Old Testament canon, which forbade adding to or subtracting from it (Deut. 4:2; 12:32). The principle applies by extension to the New Testament canon as a whole. We are not supposed to add more words or more books to the completed New Testament, because the revelation through Christ is final.

This principle has practical force. Many of the false, heretical movements in history have claimed to have extra revelations, or extra books beyond the contents of the Bible. The Mormons have their extra books. Islam has the Qur'an, which it claims is inspired.

If we are not supposed to be looking for extra books, what are we supposed to be doing? We are still supposed to be exercising spiritual gifts—that is clear. These will include prophetic, kingly, and priestly gifts. Our gifts will imitate the gifts exercised by Christ and by his apostles. They may look similar. But they will be subordinate. When properly exercised, they will acknowledge and submit to the once-for-all words of God given in Scripture, both Old Testament and New Testament.

AWARENESS OF BASIS FOR WORDS AND ACTION

We can also classify the functioning of gifts of the Spirit in another way. Let us consider a distinction that focuses on people's awareness of a basis for their ideas or actions.

At times people may consciously derive ideas for their actions from particular passages of the Bible. For example, a teacher giving an expository sermon consciously bases the sermon on one passage of the Bible. A deacon consoling someone in a personal tragedy may consciously have in mind Romans 12:15. An elder counseling a young person tempted to drunkenness may consciously base his advice on passages warning about drunkenness. Let us call this type of exercise of a gift an *inferential process*. The action is inferred from one or more passages of the Bible. The elder arrives at his words of counsel through reasoning rather than intuition.

By contrast, at other times people may act on "hunches" or "feelings" or intuition. They sense that they should say or do a particular thing. They may see a situation and spontaneously react. Or they may have special visions or auditions (hearing a voice). But in these cases they are not consciously aware of a passage of the Bible or a set of passages that forms the sole basis for their experience. Their experience springs from a personal impulse that they do not, perhaps cannot, further analyze. Let us call such instances *noninferential processes* or *intuitive processes*.

Third, people may act with partial awareness of the basis for action. For example, they compare their own situation with some model situation in the Bible. They intuitively sense that their situation is parallel to the biblical situation, but without being aware of all the factors relevant to judging the nature of the comparison. Such processes are partly inferential. We may call them *mixed processes* or *creative-discerning processes*. For many people in many situations, this third kind of mixed process may well be the most common. But for simplicity we will focus largely on the more "one-sided" processes, namely, inferential and noninferential processes.

All three of the above labels are intended to be descriptive, not evaluative. That is, we are at this point describing what various people may do, without either approving or disapproving.

We can give examples from the New Testament of all three types of processes. Most apostolic preaching involved inferential processes. "From morning till evening he [Paul] expounded to them, testifying to the kingdom of God and trying to convince them about Jesus both from the Law of Moses and from the Prophets. And some were convinced by what he said, but others disbelieved" (Acts 28:23–24). Paul relied on "the Law of Moses" and "the Prophets," which shows an inferential process. Similarly, the apostolic sermons in Acts appealed to specific texts of the Old Testament and put together arguments. The apostles endeavored to convince their hearers. People believed them not merely because they claimed to have direct divine authority, but also because people were "examining the Scriptures daily to see if these things were so" (Acts 17:11).

The visions in Revelation and elsewhere illustrate noninferential processes. John saw visions, heard voices, and recorded what he saw and heard (Rev. 22:8).

A possible instance of a mixed process, or creative-discerning process, is found in Acts 15. The apostles and elders settled a new controversy partly by creatively appealing to explicit Scriptures (Acts 15:16–18), partly by discerning an analogy between the general issue and a crucial incident that happened with Peter (15:7–11).

The boundaries of these three types of processes are fluid. We may be more or less aware of a few or many of the elements that contribute to our actions.

In the case of apostolic examples, the relevant inferential and noninferential processes are all inspired and divinely authoritative. In other cases, the processes are not inspired. In fact, they may take place under demonic influence. Satan (the chief demon) appealed to inferential reasoning in Matthew 4:6. He and his demon associates are behind false teaching according to 2 Timothy 2:26 and 1 Timothy 4:1-3, and the human false teachers may many times use (or rather misuse) inferential reasoning. In addition, demons influence noninferential processes in Ezekiel 12:24; 13:7 and Luke 4:34.

In still other cases inferential and noninferential processes operate in the normal course of human experience. For example, inferential processes are at work in Abigail's argument in 1 Samuel 25:28–31; noninferential processes dominate when David gives himself over to grief in 2 Samuel 19:4, until Joab recalls him to his duty in 2 Samuel 19:5–8. In general, there is no reason to believe that either inferential or noninferential processes are innately superior. Both may be inspired, in the case of apostolic examples, but both may also be noninspired.

How do we fit modern Christian living into this picture? Let us use the term *post-apostolic gifts* to refer to those that the Lord gives after the time of the apostles and after completion of the New Testament canon. Figure 1 suggests that we should think of post-apostolic gifts of the Spirit by analogy with gifts exercised by the apostles. Hence, in principle there is room for gifts that function as inferential processes, noninferential processes, and mixed processes. Modern examples confirm this inference. Some people are very good at building explicit arguments from the Bible. Their gifts use inferential processes. Others, through long years of studying and digesting the Bible, and through the Holy Spirit who works the knowledge of the truth in their hearts, just "know" what is right, but without being able at the moment to cite a verse justifying their conclusion. Their gifts involve noninferential processes. Others, of course, may typically be aware of some but not all biblical sources for their action. The Holy Spirit is the source of all these gifts. He works both through inferential processes and through noninferential processes.

This diversity of processes holds in particular in the area of verbal gifts or gifts of knowledge and speech, that is, prophetic as opposed to kingly and priestly gifts. Some people know and speak primarily on the basis of explicit reasoning from explicit passages of the Bible. Others know and speak on the basis of their own intuitive sense of what is in accord with the gospel (see figure 2). The distinction between inferential and noninferential speaking gifts applies now, but it is also illustrated in the time of the apostles by the difference between the Gospel of Luke and Revelation. The Holy Spirit used inferential processes in Luke to produce the Gospel, while he used noninferential (visionary) processes in producing Revelation.

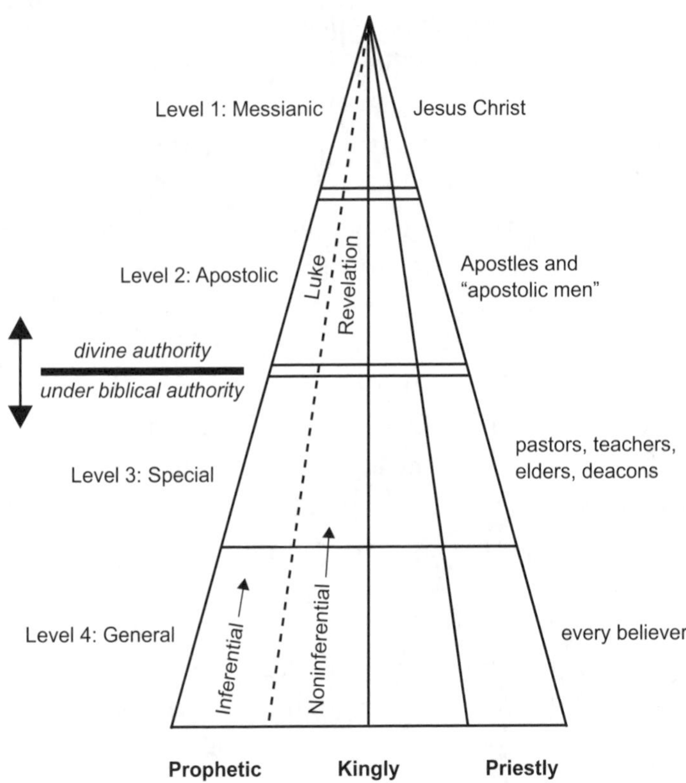

Note that within figures 1 and 2, post-apostolic gifts always belong to levels 3 and 4, which are called special gifts and general gifts. Post-apostolic gifts are all fallible. They are all dependent on Scripture and do not add to the biblical canon. They are thus analogous to but not identical with apostolic gifts (level 2) and messianic gifts (level 1).

What goes on in our times on levels 3 and 4? Inferential processes include contemporary preaching and informal Bible study and teaching. Noninferential processes include instances where biblical ideas or verses come spontaneously to mind, but without the recipient knowing just where or how they arose. Sometimes more striking instances occur. In a dream or a vision a person sees a woman in a simple white robe. She is walking through a muddy area. Some mud gets spattered on her robe. She comes to the gate of a palace. As she stands outside, she weeps with shame at her filthiness. A man comes and gives her a glorious bright gown. She puts it on and enters the palace with joy. Or a man has a dream where an angel is writing in a book. At the top of the page is the man's own name. Under it are all the evil things he has done and the evil thoughts he has entertained. A man appears with a bright face, his palms dripping with blood. He smears his hands over the page. A voice tells the angel to read what is on the page, but the angel answers, "I cannot, because it is covered with blood."

What do we think about such dreams and visions? Let us first ask ourselves a related question. Is apostolic preaching genuinely analogous to post-apostolic preaching? Certainly apostolic preaching is inspired and unique. Post-apostolic preaching does not add to apostolic preaching, but is wholly derivative from it. Hence we may perhaps hesitate to call the two "analogous." Yet in some ways the two are unmistakably analogous. Preachers and commentators have always been willing to draw lessons from the examples of the apostles and even from the example of Jesus, even though they are unique.

Similarly, we may ask whether Revelation is genuinely analogous to post-apostolic visions or dreams. The answer is similar to what we might say about preaching. Revelation is inspired and unique. Post-apostolic impressions or visions, to be valid, must not add to the Bible but be wholly derivative from it. This derivative character is in fact evident in the two instances above, with the muddy robe and the smeared book. Both contain the biblical teaching about pardon and righteousness in Christ, and both use themes and imagery derived from the Bible. The first is more general, while the second applies the truth of justification to a particular person. The second "goes beyond the Bible" only by way of its particular application, and hence everyone can recognize the legitimacy of its message. "What one person calls a 'vision' actually may have been a moving application by the Holy Spirit of the truth of Scripture to his life."[2]

People may sometimes be concerned about other distinctions. They may say, for example, that apostolic preaching and Revelation are fundamentally different because they involve new content, new revelation. By contrast, post-apostolic sermons and biblically based visions and intuitions contain a redigestion of "old truth." But the differences here, although real, are subtle and easy to exaggerate. Apostolic teaching is to a remarkable extent based on the Old Testament, the events of Christ's life, and the teaching of Jesus during his time on earth (including Luke 24:25–27, 44–49!). Thus it is far from being absolutely new, although the message may have been new to many who first heard it. The book of Revelation weaves together a remarkable amount of thematic material from Daniel, Ezekiel, Zechariah, and other biblical sources. The accounts in Luke and Acts, by recording earlier events, introduce nothing fundamentally new *in addition* to those events. Moreover, divine authority has nothing to do with whether something is old or new. Deuteronomy is just as authoritative when it repeats earlier revelation as it is when it introduces something new.

In the post-apostolic situation, preaching and visions and dreams, although old in one sense, may be new in another: they may well communicate ideas that are new *to those who receive them*. Moreover, there are always new *applications* to new persons and new circumstances (as with the man's name on the blood-smeared book).

Then where is the decisive difference? All the post-apostolic processes are wholly derivative with respect to *authority*. Post-apostolic preaching possesses authority only insofar as it reiterates the message of Scripture. The same holds for post-apostolic intuitions, dreams, visions, and all other noninferential processes.

Within this picture, we must take seriously the sufficiency of the Bible and the fallibility of post-apostolic processes. This principle holds with respect to both inferential and noninferential processes. In the case of inferential processes, a person might preach either sound doctrine or heresy. An intuitive hunch or a dream (when interpreted) might be either true or false. In a post-apostolic context, neither inferential nor noninferential processes can add teaching beyond the Bible.

To many people, a vision or audition might seem more striking and more inexplicable than the inferential processes of preaching. Hence, they reason, it is "directly" from the Holy Spirit and therefore infallible. But that is not correct. The Bible warns us that God may permit the devil to produce counterfeit miracles:

> If a prophet or a dreamer of dreams arises among you and gives you a sign or a wonder, and the sign or wonder that he tells you comes to pass, and if he says, "Let us go after other gods," which you have not known, "and let us serve them," you shall not listen to the words of that prophet or that dreamer of dreams. For the LORD your God is testing you, to know whether you love the LORD your God with all your heart and with all your soul. (Deut. 13:1–3)

> The coming of the lawless one is by the activity of Satan with all power and false signs and wonders, and

> with all wicked deception for those who are perishing, because they refused to love the truth and so be saved. (2 Thess. 2:9–10)

No post-apostolic spectacular experience, no matter how unusual or striking, can fundamentally add to the Bible. It may in fact be a counterfeit miracle, in the sense of 2 Thessalonians 2:9–11; or it may be a reiteration of biblical truth, yet still contaminated by sinful human reception; or it may contain information about the present situation (see below); or it may be a confused mixture of truth and error. We test all such experience using the Bible as our infallible standard.

DISTINCTIVE FOCUSES FOR CONTENT

We need one final distinction, one with respect to *content* rather than *process*. So far we have been talking about the process by which people come to say something. But we must also attend to the content of what they say. This content may represent an attempt to reexpress the content of Scripture, or it may be an attempt to say something about the circumstances around us, or it may be a combination of both.

First, people may speak with a focus on didactic content. They tell us what they think the Bible teaches or what they think God commands. "God wants us to pray for the sick." Let us call the content of such speech *teaching content*.

Second, people may speak with a focus on circumstances. They tell us what is happening around them. Or they tell what has happened in the past or (if they predict something) what will happen. "Someone here has back trouble." Let us call such speech *circumstantial content*.

Third, people may speak with a content that aims to combine biblical teaching and circumstantial information. People tell us how they think the Bible applies to the current situation. "We need to pray for so-and-so who has back trouble." Let us call such speech *applicatory content*.

Within the New Testament, whatever Jesus and the apostles teach is the word of God. Thus it is teaching content, whether it focally speaks of God or history or their circumstances or application. Then where does circumstantial content come in? It enters when we attempt to apply the Bible to our own circumstances. The New Testament commands us to apply this Word in a discerning way in our own lives, where we continually confront new circumstances and new challenges (Rom. 12:1–2; Eph. 5:16–17). To accomplish this application, we must inevitably deal with circumstantial and applicatory content.

Now the Bible is the foundation for exercising godly discernment about our circumstances. The teaching of the Bible is thus foundational in the Holy Spirit's work of teaching today. But there is reason to believe that the Holy Spirit as Creator and Redeemer is involved as well in the mundane aspects of our learning about ourselves and our circumstances (Job 32:8; Ps. 94:10; Prov. 1:2–7). As Proverbs 2:6 indicates, "the LORD gives wisdom; from his mouth come knowledge and understanding." This knowledge from the Lord includes the wisdom and insight concerning everyday life that the rest of the book of Proverbs champions. Everyday knowledge, as well as the explicit teaching of the Bible, comes from the Lord.

Today's circumstances do not of course possess any special authority. The Bible, by contrast, possesses divine authority. Hence, on the issue of authority there is a great gulf between today's circumstances and the Bible's statements about circumstances of biblical times. But in another sense there is an obvious relationship. The people in biblical times had problems, struggles, and circumstances like ours. In some ways, then, their application of more general biblical principles to their circumstances parallels our application of the Bible to our own new circumstances. In all cases the Lord is involved in instructing us. It is he who gives us both knowledge of biblical principles and knowledge of the circumstances to which we must respond.

THE QUESTION OF CHARISMATIC GIFTS

We can now integrate contemporary gifts into our general framework. In our day, various kinds of gifts function through various processes. It is unnecessary to note them all. The more controversial kinds of gifts need our attention, in particular the verbal gifts that "charismatic" groups classify as instances of a word of knowledge, a word of wisdom, prophecy, discerning spirits, tongues, and interpretation of tongues.

Those in the charismatic movement believe that the gifts of prophecy, discernment of spirits, and tongues continue in the church today, while others argue that they ceased with the ministry of the apostles and the completion of special revelation. Our investigation of the Bible suggests that post-apostolic gifts are *analogous* to inspired apostolic gifts. Hence it may or may not be appropriate to call them by the same *terms* as those used in the New Testament. Rather than becoming bogged down in disputes about terminology, let us move directly to consideration of what the post-apostolic gifts actually do within the framework of figure 2.

In terms of our earlier classification, all these controversial gifts are noninferential processes. They are controversial because their basis is more obscure and more private. That is, the basis is noninferential or "intuitive." By contrast, inferential processes are uncontroversial, because they appeal to the Bible.

According to the theology of spiritual gifts, inferential and noninferential gifts simply stand alongside all other gifts, with no particular superiority. Like all gifts, they are to be checked for conformity to Scripture (1 Cor. 14:37–38).

But should these noninferential cases even be called "gifts" of the Holy Spirit? We have already observed from Job 32:8; Psalm 94:10; and Proverbs 2:6 that the Holy Spirit as Creator and Sustainer of human life gives people all the knowledge that they have. So in a broad sense these are "gifts." Moreover, by labeling these works "gifts" we do not attribute to them infallibility. A gift in preaching, although it be genuine, does not give the contemporary preacher infallibility, because the gift operates in the midst of human sin and bias; the same is true for noninferential gifts.

Some people still have problems with noninferential processes because, they would claim, they are innately uncheckable. If no one can tell whether they conform to Scripture, then they threaten to disturb the exclusive role that the Bible plays in the church's foundation.

But not every instance of noninferential processes is equally a problem. We need to consider separately teaching content and circumstantial content.

Teaching content is like an extemporaneous sermon without a text. If the process is noninferential, the speaker is not consciously aware of texts on which the speech is based. But even if the *speaker* is not consciously aware of texts, the *listeners* may become conscious of texts that are relevant. If the content is biblical, such texts do exist. If the content is not biblical, then the speech is not to be believed. Hence, this type of content is testable. Anyone who knows the Bible well, or knows the gospel, can see whether the message matches what he knows. Many utterances called "prophecies" string together biblical phraseology. It is not too hard to see their generally biblical character.

It is, of course, a little easier to evaluate a textually based sermon. The text is explicit, and the listeners have immediate access to it. They can compare the text with what the preacher says. But there are still difficulties. A clever heretic may use a text plausibly. And a non-heretical preacher may find himself drifting away from the text by design or on the spur of the moment. Discernment is therefore necessary in evaluating teaching content, no matter whether the process involved is inferential or noninferential.

Note also that people differ in the ways they exercise discernment. For some people, discernment may usually be inferential. In their minds they remember a biblical text that conforms with what the preacher says or else contradicts it. Other people may discern noninferentially. They "feel" that what the preacher is saying is right or wrong. They cannot point to a specific text. But they just know, perhaps on the basis of having assimilated and digested a large amount of the Bible. Their digested knowledge now works in their hearts "subconsciously" to give them discernment. The thought spontaneously rises in their minds, "Something is wrong with this message."

Since the Holy Spirit is at work in the lives of believers, we may also describe all these processes as *Spirit-worked*. Of course the Holy Spirit works in ways we cannot fathom. But he *also* works through means, such as our knowledge of Scripture, a knowledge that he has produced (1 Cor. 2:10–16). From the human side people use primarily inferential or noninferential processes. But this human description does not contradict the fact that the Spirit is working. (Again, think of the example of the Gospel of Luke and the book of Revelation.)

Different types of people help one another. Occasionally a person who discerns inferentially may not immediately think of a relevant biblical text to use in evaluating a message. But someone else feels intuitively that something is wrong. Then the person with inferential discernment takes more time, and finally a text does come to mind that helps judge the truth of the speaker's message.

CIRCUMSTANTIAL CONTENT RECEIVED THROUGH NONINFERENTIAL PROCESSES

So far, we have discussed teaching content. This kind of content is the easiest. Let us now consider the second kind of content, namely, circumstantial content. In this category we have statements like the following. In an American church someone says, "I feel that our sister church in Shanghai is spiritually struggling and undergoing attack." During a sermon Charles H. Spurgeon "pointed to the gallery and said, 'Young man, the gloves in your pocket are not paid for.' "[3] On another occasion Spurgeon said, "There is a man sitting there who is a shoemaker; he keeps his shop open on Sundays; it was open last Sabbath morning. He took ninepence, and there was fourpence profit on it: his soul is sold to Satan for fourpence!"[4] A woman in Switzerland saw a vision of a lecture hall in Essex, in which Os Guinness was about to lecture. A strange girl was about to disrupt the meeting.[5] All these are cases of circumstantial content obtained through noninferential processes.

This kind of content can undoubtedly create difficulty. But the difficulties diminish if we realize that this information is not very different *in content* from information obtained through obvious channels. For example, in principle the church in Shanghai might have been able to put in a phone call to the brothers and sisters in the United States. Spurgeon could have obtained the information (but did not) from the person who stole the gloves or from the person who opened his shop on Sunday. Os Guinness could have called the woman in Switzerland. The kind of information involved is not striking. What is striking is that the information came through *noninferential processes*. There was no obvious long-distance call or other scientifically analyzable means that could account for how the information came to the recipient.

In terms of figure 2, such information is a product of spiritual processes operating on the level of the ordinary believer (level 4), or conceivably on the level of "special gifts" (level 3). Since the canon is complete, there is no way that this information belongs on level 1 or level 2. Moreover, there is no practical reason why the information *needs* to belong to level 1 or level 2. What matters is that the recipients received information, not that the information had some special status. Hence, information of this kind belongs to the same broad category as information received through telephone calls, newspaper news, and direct observation. It is simply information about the world, not more, not less. In principle, it is no more a threat to the sufficiency of Scripture than is information about whether I brushed my teeth after breakfast!

How do we evaluate circumstantial content? Suppose someone claims that the church in Shanghai is under spiritual attack? Are we to believe the claim or not? Many times it does not much matter what we believe. We are free to remain in doubt. And we are well advised to remain in doubt, by virtue of the fallibility of all post-apostolic noninferential processes. We can pray for a situation without knowing for certain whether the situation is exactly what we think it is. We can pray for the sister church in Shanghai.

In actuality we are accustomed in many types of situations to respond to doubtful information. After all, a long-distance call is not infallible either. There may be static on the line. The person on the other end of the line may have misunderstood the situation in Shanghai. Or he may be lying about the situation. In spite of these problems of fallibility, it is possible to respond properly to a long-distance call.

SPEAKING IN TONGUES

Finally, what should we think about speaking in tongues? The Bible discusses the subject in Acts 2:1–12; 10:46; 19:6; and 1 Corinthians 12:10, 28, 30; 13:1, 8; 14:1–40. Tongues are closely linked to prophesying. It appears that in Acts 2 the apostles spoke in languages that their hearers understood. In the Corinthian church, speaking in tongues sounded like languages, but the hearers and even the speakers usually did not recognize the language. The speeches had to be interpreted in order to be understood (1 Cor. 14:2–6, 13, 27–28). When they were interpreted, they built up the church in the same way as prophesying (1 Cor. 14:5).

According to 1 Corinthians, speaking in tongues is one spiritual gift among many (1 Cor. 12:10, 28–30). Some but not all Christians have the gift (1 Cor. 12:30). In the twentieth century, however, some people began to claim that every Christian ought to speak in tongues as the sign of being baptized with the Holy Spirit. They postulated a distinction between the "sign" of tongues, which they claimed was for everyone, and the "gift" of tongues, which they admitted was only for some Christians.

This thinking is muddled. As we indicated earlier, every Christian believer receives the indwelling of the Holy Spirit when he receives Christ. Every gift of the Holy Spirit is a sign of his indwelling. In addition, 1 Corinthians 14:22, in the context of its discussion of the *gift* of tongues, says that "tongues are a *sign*." The two terms—*gift* and *sign*—act as two labels for the same reality. In Acts, tongues and prophecy and miracles and the powerful preaching of the gospel all function in a broad sense as *signs* or indications of the Spirit at work. Acts 2 mentions tongues, but also indicates that the speakers proclaimed "the mighty works of God," a form of prophesying (Acts 2:11). Peter's sermon to the people also shows the Holy Spirit powerfully at work (Acts 2:14–41).

Acts pays special attention to tongues because Pentecost marks the beginning of a new era in God's plan. The multiple languages show that now the Word of God is going to spread to all the nations of the world, rather than being confined to Palestine and the Israelite nation (Acts 1:8). The inclusion of all the nations fulfills the prophecy in Joel 2:28–29, quoted in Acts 2:17–18: the Spirit will be poured out "on all flesh."

Does the gift of speaking in tongues fit into the overall pattern of spiritual gifts, as summarized in figure 2? It does. Speaking is a prophetic gift. Speaking in tongues, when interpreted, functions like prophesying, and prophesying belongs with other prophetic functions. Figure 2 suggests that tongues can occur at an inspired, apostolic level. The apostle Paul indicates that he spoke in tongues (1 Cor. 14:18). That level is now complete, because of the completion of the canon of the New Testament. But tongues can also occur at a subordinate level, the "general" level of every believer. When a missionary brings the gospel to people in a language that he has learned, he is using his speaking gift *inferentially*. If a person speaks in tongues and does not know the full meaning of what he says, he is speaking *noninferentially*. The same could hold for a person who undertakes to interpret. An interpreter could function *inferentially* if he recognizes the language. Or he could function *noninferentially*, if he does not directly recognize words and sentences, but God nevertheless gives him some grasp of what is said. As a church we should evaluate all such communications using the Bible as our standard, just as we would do for any other speech.

When someone speaks in tongues privately, he is praying or praising God (1 Cor. 14:2, 14, 16). God understands, even though no one else does (1 Cor. 14:2). Speaking in tongues publicly is appropriate only if it can be interpreted, so the church as a whole can be built up (1 Cor. 14:16–17, 26).

WELCOMING SPIRITUAL GIFTS

Let us return to the main point. In our day, God may work through both inferential and noninferential processes. In the time of the apostles, both kinds of processes occurred in inspired form. In our time, the giving of the canon of Scripture is complete and inspiration has ceased. Post-apostolic processes are fallible. But they are *analogous* to the processes that occurred among the apostles. In understanding post-apostolic spiritual gifts, we are to take our cue from what happened in apostolic times.

What, then, are we to do about spiritual gifts in our time? Contemporary gifts include both inferential (for example, teaching) and noninferential kinds (for example, the ability to give an apt word spontaneously, Col. 4:6). The possibility of both kinds of gifts can be inferred from the analogous distribution of different kinds of gifts in the time of the apostles. Moreover, Christ and the Holy Spirit are the source of all gifts (Eph. 4:7, 11; see also 1 Cor. 12:11). It is they, not we, who decide when to use inferential and noninferential processes as the Holy Spirit works.

In response, we are to welcome spiritual gifts of all kinds, honor them, and receive them (1 Cor. 12:14–26). We are especially to pursue love (1 Cor. 13) and those gifts that build up the church (1 Cor. 14). At the same time, we are to be discriminating (1 Thess. 5:21–22). We are to exercise discernment. Postapostolic manifestations are always fallible. Everything is to be evaluated on the basis of Scripture, to which nothing is to be added at any time (Deut. 4:2; Rev. 22:18–19).

FOR FURTHER READING

Clowney, Edmund P. *The Church*. Downers Grove, IL: InterVarsity, 1995.

Ferguson, Sinclair B. *The Holy Spirit*. Downers Grove, IL: InterVarsity, 1996.

Gaffin, Richard B. Jr. *Perspectives on Pentecost: Studies in New Testament Teaching on the Gifts of the Holy Spirit*. Grand Rapids: Baker, 1979.

Packer, J. I. *Keep in Step with the Spirit: Finding Fullness in Our Walk with God*. Grand Rapids: Baker, 2005.

Poythress, Vern S. "Linguistic and Sociological Analyses of Modern Tongues-Speaking: Their Contributions and Limitations," *Westminster Theological Journal* 42/2 (1980): 367–88. http://www.frame-poythress.org/poythress_articles/1980Linguistic.htm.

__________. "Modern Spiritual Gifts as Analogous to Apostolic Gifts: Affirming Extraordinary Works of the Spirit within Cessationist Theology," *Journal of the Evangelical Theological Society* 39/1 (1996): 71–101. Available at <http://www.frame-poythress.org/poythress_articles/1996Modern.htm>.

__________. "The Nature of Corinthian Glossolalia: Possible Options," *Westminster Theological Journal* 40/1 (1977): 130–35. http://www.frame-poythress.org/poythress_articles/1977Nature.htm.

Ridderbos, Herman N. *Redemptive History and the New Testament Scriptures*. Phillipsburg, NJ: Presbyterian and Reformed, 1988.

NOTES

1. O. Palmer Robertson, *The Final Word: A Biblical Response to the Case for Tongues and Prophecy Today* (Carlisle, PA: The Banner of Truth Trust, 1993), 84.
2. Ernest W. Bacon, *Spurgeon: Heir of the Puritans* (Grand Rapids: Eerdmans, 1968), 156.
3. Ibid.
4. Os Guinness, *The Dust of Death* (Downers Grove: InterVarsity, 1973), 299.